MID/SOUTH
SONNETS

T0307170

MID/SOUTH SONNETS

A BELLE POINT PRESS ANTHOLOGY

EDITED BY C. T. SALAZAR & CASIE DODD

BELLE
POINT
PRESS

Fort Smith, Arkansas

MID/SOUTH SONNETS

Edited by C. T. Salazar & Casie Dodd
Design & typography by Belle Point Press

© 2023 Belle Point Press, LLC
Fort Smith, Arkansas
bellepointpress.com
editor@bellepointpress.com

Cover Image: Sanborn Fire Insurance Map from
Fort Smith, Sebastian County, Arkansas, October 1901.
Interior cover images: Sanborn Fire Insurance Maps from
Greenville, Washington County, Mississippi, September 1896
and from Memphis, Shelby County, Tennessee, 1897.
Library of Congress via Wikimedia Commons.

Find Belle Point Press
on Facebook,
Twitter (@BellePointPress),
and Instagram (@bellepointpress)

Printed in the United States of America

27 26 25 24 23   1 2 3 4 5

Library of Congress Control Number: 2023942158

ISBN: 978-1-960215-04-8

MSA02/BPP14

Contents

Publisher's Note

When we published the first *Mid/South Anthology* last year, my husband and I had no idea what to expect. It was a leap of faith into the publishing world that has rewarded us with new relationships and the momentum to start building this press into something that we hope will last.

This time around, I felt more confident, largely thanks to the friendship and direction of C. T. Salazar. As soon as I landed on the idea of sonnets as the next anthology's focus, C. T. was the obvious choice to help form this project into something more fully representative of the in-betweenness of the Mid-South, the Delta, and the expansiveness of Southern culture. C. T.'s roots in the region made me feel right at home developing this collection with him, and I'm forever grateful for—and immensely proud of—what we've put together.

The sonnet felt right for a poetry anthology because it remains tethered to a tradition while continually shaping itself to match the experiences that inspire it. In *Mid/South Sonnets*, you'll find familiar and surprising approaches to the form, though they largely share a common goal in navigating home and the people who make (or break) us. While Belle Point Press remains committed to seeking and nurturing the creative lives of writers who choose to maintain their homes *here*, in and around this place—the Mid-South—in this collection we were struck by the range of people who either continue to feel a sense of belonging here after they leave or who decide to stick around after coming from elsewhere. The sonnet offers a similar flexibility, rooted in the universal process of struggling through something broken to emerge a little more formed, even if not entirely whole.

Thank you for reading. Come find us where the rivers meet.

CASIE DODD
The Arkansas River Valley, May 2023

Introduction

Discourse on what constitutes a sonnet is no doubt as friction-filled as the question of what constitutes the South. Like the endless variations and repetitions of landscapes, history, and personhood that make this place, C. F. Johnson tells us "Sonnet beauty depends on symmetry and asymmetry both. . . . It resembles things of organic beauty as opposed to things of geometric beauty."* Part of its allure—for me—is how moving through the form so closely mimics how time and space are experienced, briefly. Recently I had the opportunity to walk some of the fields I was raised around. I forgot the feeling that comes with crossing from the field into the woodline. How the world changes all at once, just like that. In the woods even the temperature was different. Where in the vast open I was the tallest thing, now the world was above me and all sides were singing down instead of just under me. I didn't know this change was coming, and I didn't know until I was already in that change how I would experience it. In the field or in the woods—I was on either side of a volta.

A volta isn't just a turn, but a transformation. What a sonnet does best is offer us a moment of transformation; that at any place in the poem we are navigating an unlocated present, either about to experience this change or having just met the consequences of it. A language of moment where we can be changed and enact change in a way that shows the true interdependence between our attention and our world.

* "Forms of Poetry," 1904.

Even as this unlocated mode is poetic and sublime, I think there's an obligation to ground this introduction, to tell you about some of the things that are shaping the South as I've been writing this. To *locate* this present and the context I'm writing within. In the Mississippi Delta where I am, a record-breaking EF4 tornado carved a sixty-mile-long scar across the land, destroying several towns. And the same has just happened in Arkansas. In Atlanta, activists are doing everything they can to halt the 90-million-dollar construction of Cop City, an 85-acre militarized facility for the Atlanta Police Department. In Tennessee, three state legislators faced expulsion for participating in protests on gun reform with their constituents. The Don't Say Gay bill (Florida Parental Rights in Education Act) and the Anti-Immigration bill (SB 1718) are enacted in Florida. Across almost every state in the South, anti-Trans legislature is filling the governing halls of power, threatening the lives and liberties of our neighbors, our beloveds. Unalienable reproductive rights have been taken away. Every day, Black and Brown men and women are harmed by the still-alive faucets of Jim Crow, whose pulse can be measured in the South's incarceration statistics, housing inequity, and every other nameable aspect of our daily social strata.

This list goes on, but I wanted you to know where I am. Gwendolyn Brooks says, "The whirlwind is our commonwealth."* It's through these pressures and many more that the poets in this anthology are working. Diana E. Henderson captures the historic way sonnets allow a poet to respond to their own time:

> The sonnet form originated in an age when poets were also political "subjects" to princes, when emotions were perceived as external forces pressuring internal spirits and when earthly experience was deemed

---

* "The Second Sermon on the Warpland."

subject to heavenly will; the sonnet allowed poets a fourteen-line space in which they could at least articulate, if not exert, their own wills.[*]

We are made neighbors not just by our geography, but of all the contentions, consequences, and beauty that build, reinforce, and break the South. Many times over, the sixty-six poets presented show us the relative arbitrariness of the lines drawn: the ways the South and its products are entangled to the Global South and fundamentally to the entire world in past, present, future. In the thick of it all, we have prepared a table. But because I'm terrified of being seen as one thing and one thing only, I'm hesitant to simply describe the poets in this anthology as southerners. The sonnets within these pages show us deeply beautiful and complex interior lives across a multitude of identity. Lyric selves filled with joy, oppression, resistance, ambition, precarity, and wonder. Can all of this be feasibly hemmed in by the single word—*southerner*?

I entered each of these sonnets and came out something else. I recognized places, and I found myself in entirely unfamiliar surroundings. These sonnets upend a status quo. Their speakers mourn and love in deeply radical ways. In "An Intact World," Rita Dove's introductory essay to her collection of sonnets *Mother Love*, she asks, "Can't form also be a talisman against disintegration?" The work in this anthology fulfills the validity of this question by showing how many other things "form" could be instead, while still staying true to the question. The sonnet lets us also ask: can't loving be a talisman against disintegration? Can't screaming? Remembering? Neighborliness? What the sonnet reveals to us is how many of our practices are both commonplace and history-surviving.

---

[*] "The Sonnet, Subjectivity, and Gender."

It can never be said we weren't here; as Gwendolyn Brooks put it, here's the record of our living in the "noise and whip of the whirlwind."

Making this book with Casie has been one of the most fulfilling moments in poetry for me yet. Every conversation we had around making this anthology made me sharper. Michael's labor in the design and production of this project into a physical book is endlessly applause-worthy. Lastly, I am deeply grateful and in awe of the sixty-six poets that make this book what it is. You affirm my joy, and you make this place possible. There are so many incredible southern poets writing sonnets, and this anthology is far from exhaustive. Rather, it represents a single moment in which poets hailing from or living in the South across a spectrum of race, class, gender, ability, and age all said *here I am.*

C. T. SALAZAR
The Mississippi Delta, June 2023

Carthage

Now the fog rolls in like fallen clouds,
clings to potholes in clay roads and we
pretend we're in a field, stretched on our backs:
the symmetry of sadness. We intuit stories

from the mist. There, a crystal glass
of steaming mint tea above the ghostly
minarets reflected on the sea. No.
We are also rubble: empty citadels

with shuttered windows and welcome mats charred.
I tell you the myth of a goddess who held a sword
halted before her throat. She thought it foolish
to die for this. Now, I'm the one asking

us to leave: a thousand ships with burning
sails, spirits sowing these fields with salt.

The Reasons We're Falling Apart

Because the crops failed, the tax
on farm animals was raised
a few percent, the handle of our ax
fell off as we chopped. We praised
God every Sunday but still lost
the farm when the rain stopped.
Last winter, that goddamn frost.
It killed all the crops. Dropped
our ploughs. There's nothing to plant,
& there's nothing to eat—
we were waiting on a grant
that'll never come. Our bare feet
caked with dirt, the soles turned black.
The truck engine's cracked.

ANNA LENA PHILLIPS BELL

August, Nantahala National Forest

Past dark, collecting water, high in a hollow,
there in my flashlight's beam: a salamander
so big—span of my hand—still in the shallows,
skin river-gold, one eye on me—*hellbender*,
I thought. This was its stream. I should have known
that afternoon, when I walked down the glen
and jumped and hollered in the cold—not mine.
Giddy before I'd even gotten in,
worldbender, waterbender, splitting the gap
with splash and screech, oblivious, filled to full—
the hell in me is that I'd do it again,
in leafy sun, in nothing, toe-heel down
the sand to stand waist deep in the ancient pool,
laugh and leap up, leap up, leap up, leap up—

Double Sonnet Instead of an Introduction

Instead of your name, the barista writes *Eden*
across the flat white you drink and you drink
hours after the yawn of daybreak has closed
its mouth. And what of it? Error, as you well
know, began the new world. Your ancestors
shifted the vowels of your surname: an *i*
giving way to *y*. The whirr of a milk frother.

Nearly every continent is in your genealogy:
You are Black. You come from a Creole
so old no one can skin the pear of your first
language. The whole of the Gulf rests
in your spit. You are Afro-Latino and know
so little Spanish. Shame scratches its forehead
when you speak or don't speak. Seven

great uncles named for conquistador resistors.
Two great aunts named for precious stones.
Onyx in one eye. Jade in the other. You worship
differently than your Catholic grandparents.
Raised in a tune up of a Black organ, you shout.
Your last name derives from Levi. The fricatives
of priesthood and Torah are all that are left. Your son

can climb one branch up the family tree and see
Scotland and Germany. His middle name is Japanese.
What even is a race? Confetti after the parade.
Night cuts its King cake into dawn, but dawn
doesn't arrive. Your mother throws a fistful of nutmeg
into the bechamel, but y'all cannot stop
arguing over what is white.

ANN FISHER-WIRTH

Buttercups, Bluets, Spring Ephemerals

St. Peter's graveyard, Oxford

In the sleepy heaviness of impending rain,
small flowers blanket the graveyard where the dead
ripen toward bone—mothers and stillborn babies,
ne'er-do-wells whose families stitched their mouths shut,
those whose markers are crosses and angels—
and the famous writer who said he just
wrote down the voices. Every day a coin
against oblivion, I thought, walking past,
and then wondered what I meant—whose eyes
are sealed with coins, whose hands would offer silver
so that we might remember, or whose tongue
receive the host in the sacrament of pain?
Or are the coins these scattered flowers—
these buttercups, bluets, spring ephemerals?

Ana Drives Me to Whipple Creek

She was like   someone   sitting down
            to play the piano   in another room
    inside   my grandmother's trailer
        showing how well   gone   can be pulled
through you   if it isn't just grief but   more like a choir.
    A truth can be   so long and so   unendearing—
we only come to look   when we're   heavy.
        What is loving   if not a face   that goes on and on   like
a landline stretched all the way from the kitchen, through a hallway,
across   a lap.   She was a voice that   could last
        longer than I could   Listen:
I was in the car,   and then I was   left-center
        being played   deep.   I was chewing thin leather
    and breathing her air   like   a tomb.

BETHANY JARMUL

My 9-Year-Old Self Dreams of Success while Stringing Green Beans

Owning a garage, especially with two stalls,
a refrigerator that makes ice, a dress from
J. C. Penney's at full price, ordering Coke
at a restaurant, Captain Crunch cereal,
American Girl dolls, Barbie houses,
new tennis shoes, anything not handed down,
riding an escalator, three-story or six-story
buildings, light-up billboards, a store I've
only heard about called Macy's. Living
in a city, nearby a city, driving to a city, visiting, touring,
vacationing, bragging about having seen, entered, lived in
something called a city. I'll be a famous movie star
when grown-up me lives there; I'll own a purse-sized chihuahua
with her own ice maker in our two-stall garage.

Talking with Thunder

Did you hear that thunder I asked. Yes and I
wonder which foot it is coming out from under
you replied. I am always working to transmute
your music into my own the thunder said. For
anybody who has not yet heard of it transmutation
means change in ways like form or nature or
substance or state. Will we be more aware once

you've done your thing to our thing we asked.
I don't know the thunder said. I am merely a
mountain of sound and sometimes things like
rain or wind transmute me. It's nothing personal
since I've never met them. What kind of logic
is that I said. If you were a mountain of sound
you'd understand the thunder said through us.

Sagittarius A*

I have not said anything worth more than a bowl of cold,
sweet watermelon in May. I have only flapped my gums
instead of flapping my arms to make of them wings. Owl wings
carry their attendant hunters on a silence so silent
it can't be real—where are the puppeteers, the thin strings
suspending the predator as it glides through whale-dark night.
Who is puppeting the whale as it breaches, as it beaches
itself on a five-star shore, as people approach it
with their hatchet hearts, with their hearts' guardrails bent and busted,
I have not said anything worth more than the eye of a whale
suspended in the body's fallen skyscraper of rot.
Used to be our buildings pointed to heaven. Heaven
turned out to be larger and hungrier than we could
possibly imagine. Our father, to eat is to exist.

RASHA ABDULHADI

Counterpoint to an Insect Collection

These painted bodies, crackle and click of shell,
soft powder on the wing, sting in the belly—
They bite skin, scurry floor, are drawn
to your porchlight but not to you. leave Them be,
These bodies ecology, They not jewel, not nature the painter
making mosaics you capture and frame. don't clip the spiderthread
tethering Their thin legjoints to This earth.

already the insects are disappearing from us,
hymenoptera, lepidoptera, mariposa, the beetles.
even the worms are making their exodus, and with them
go our immune system. look, it is happening here,
as grasping for their beauty, you lose their alliance
and such allies we will need. every body large and small
a filter cartridge for the burden we dump into the world.

What Claims Wolves Laid upon My Body

what claims wolves laid
that summer so queered
one boy after another
in one place, one foot
arriving, one hand in
one cooling grip, mouth
upon the body
the way urge begets
a child, more, more, more
how a fire chooses
the quickness of wolves
where wolves fleshed flesh
which grew me even
under oaks, under dark,
upon my body
so hot, thick with youth
i could hardly stay
departing before
the exit, one hand warm,
learning one lesson
eager for more more
the urge, emptiness
doubling desire
love's love, air, air, breath
restricting my throat
unlearning all green growth
in pain, more and more
wolves claimed me

Mush

In this place you have the mind and body of a boy,
heavy with the oils of mountain and first kiss: your responsibilities.
But you pretend more weight in the thought of leaving school.

Your mother won't let you drop out for "what work for whose money?"
though there is nothing for breakfast but corn-meal mush and sugar
which has thickened into the worst enemy of her family's mornings.

Your younger brother is refusing to finish his mush
so he will eat it for lunch, and he will not have mashed potatoes
and that is that. To prove his sincerity, he runs to the toilet and vomits.

In this place it is not your brother's misery over corn-meal mush
making you desire what has already come. Work means eating
frosted corn flakes for breakfast, like your father at his new house.

For now you must go to school. You lift and push open the screen door,
the hinges rusted half-way gone. Daddy used pine scraps. They are rotting.

My Mother Tries to Teach Me How to Pray

When I fold my hands together, I do not think
of my childhood bedtime ritual: doubling my small

body under yours to kneel where you were kneeling
to ask the Lord that we might live another day. When

I fold my hands together I do not think of you, but of
an almost-lover who folded sheets of paper into birds.

Dear dove he'd say, kneeling beside me as I closed
my eyes to stars and let him bend me into the poems

he tucked inside his pocket. Unlike other mothers,
you never asked me to close my eyes when I prayed.

Even then you must have known the fear I had—not
of darkness—but of sudden light, the knowledge that

everything is made to disappear. When I kneel, I think
of begging for my life, have learned to call this *prayer.*

My Mother Tries to Teach Me about Language

after Natasha Trethewey

All things begin with a single word.
This time, the word is a name.

> The time I defile God's name,
> you resolve to put an end to my cursing.

You resolve to put an end to my cursing
by filling my mouth with soap.

> The soap fills my mouth with sweet olive
> and cleans me from the inside out.

To be cleansed from the inside out
is the reason we drink wine at church.

> Now I drink wine to forget the Church,
> rinse my mouth with the blood of its hurt.

Rinsing my mouth of blood, I forget why I hurt.
It must have begun with a single word.

A Sonnet, Because I Didn't Want to Say, "I Already Knew"

I stood in an evening-scrubbed field. Fireflies blinked
through the eyes of every summer I didn't
share with someone I missed. There was a fence,
two dark lines and the suggestion of breaching.
When I felt the suggestion of closeness. I birthed
a question. She answered, her mouth a line of darkness.
I let her untruth me across the distance.
Her voice was every summer we didn't share,
which was every summer. In between the seasons
lies the same field. What is truth. A blink in the evening
rather than a wall of light. I forgive the distance necessary
to breach the unvoiced. When we saw the fence was
    no wall, only darkness breaching, she said, "I lied to you,"
    and I told her, "It's still a season for fireflies"

DAVID GREENSPAN

Now is what has happened

If you yourself are hell   tell me something
about thighs   about blackberries
fermenting on the porch   my hands push through
salmon, chicken's liver   what do you mean
knock, knock   I've never been able to
make heads nor tails of jokes   I've never
met a plant I didn't want to drown   if you need proof
consider the bird   sewing needled
along my knee   it's purple   smells like vinegar
when there's a chance of rain   now the power cuts
everything spoils   even squash from a neighbor's yard
as it rains & rains   we sit watching   the storm tire
all the trees   look like children
all the children   look like trees

Conway

The back-up chop of a bulking behemoth—
modern ugly and super-sized—breaks the stillness
of an era in which I am the only human moth
awake. Night-stuck, everywhere in cold recess
worse than cool; not yet frozen but near the tipping
point. A cat could die. The fleas already
have. Not a single living light is tripping.
No one's here to accompany me against the piti-
lessness. Not even mustard. Or a shoeshine.
I sit as the last living human in historical time.
I circle and wait. I debate as to where
the pup's lost, the star has gone. Readers are nowhere.
I write the little history here, this recorder's shibboleth.
They don't worry about audience; they want to tell the death.

ANDREA BLANCAS BELTRAN

Border Sonnet: Special Census of the Population of El Paso, Tex. January 15, 1916*

for my great-great-grandfather Alberto
after Lyrae Can Clief-Stefanon's "Sea Sonnet: Dakar, 2018"

Tell me, were you Contreras or Contesas then?
I cannot follow names, the full census is hidden.
1: Excluding Mexican. 2: Including Mex-
I cannot comprehend the footnoted text.
Color? Race? City reports will enumerate:
1916 (excluding Mexican) [your fate]
1910 (including Mexican) [goes here]
1900 (including Mexican), the years
oscillate when it comes to Mexican or White.
One term races the other. Definitions indict—
nothing new. Who are you? Designation's a game.
SEX: COLOR OR RACE: SEX AND AGE: marks on a page.
Dirty, lousey: the mayor's vocabulary.
No one knows how to spell your name. Reports vary.

---

* To be read forward and backward.

For My Father

after Emily Dickinson's Envelope Poems

Daddy driving us along lush levee
Mississippi River devouring eroded shores
Daddy tells his childhood histories
under rushing water, Memphis candy in
my mouth listening to the rumble of his Dodge.
Twenty years since we left the Delta
Recapturing Grandmother's ghost in
September heat, Tom Petty crooning as
I write essays for university admission.
Fateful phone call from Daddy freshman year
Absolution across the hours and tears
This poem is not enough to bare your hands
Delighting in holding my daughters at birth
Hands written in our records; hands held always.

Oblivion Sonnet, November 2020

We'll have to pack our things and leave this place
one day. The creek and beeches, half-alive,
the corkscrew roads. Maybe I'll shave my face
how you like and we can go for a drive
into town for the night. Maybe I've loved
watching the last of the fire split to embers
too much—and this blue smoke rising above
us in the sky, coupling with the new dark
in silence. Love has whittled me to me.
When I was younger and green with trouble
I envisioned my years unbound and free
from commitment. It was impossible
to imagine a life not all my own.
A runagate, wildfire and ash, windblown.

MARCUS WICKER

First Contact: ATLien Observes Love

My existence here evidences man's belief   in dreams   Man's capacity
to forgive   its self-evident sins   of which   & according to their text histories

are many   My existence here may be forgiven   figuring man's entertainment
systems   their content-aggregating mobile applications   [you'd like them]

Was at Chicken + Beer   swallowing fried scents   cataloging   returning the
bounce &   healing nod of African Americans when   witnessed in   tender palms

a square parable generator   showing one gladiator   batter another's eardrum
A little riffle rushing from his canal   The maniacal one   draping staff arms

around his adversary's shoulders   over springy red ropes   Lapping at the carnage
w/ a pink algae tongue   If telegenic violence deafens humans from bloodguilt

then i find solace in its opposite   at the Hartsfield-Jackson launchpad   when a brown
girl grazes her elbow at my table's ragged edge   &   as infant kin kisses beaded striation

i feel it   infecting my capillaries   This saccharine contaminant   Ultra HD
streaming thru ventricles & fountain machine tributaries   into whosoever drinks

MARCUS WICKER

ATLien Considers Neighborliness as a Conditional Concept

Judge Lets Derek Chauvin, Ex-Cop Charged in George Floyd's Death, Live Out of State after Posting Bond
            —Steve Karnowski, Associated Press

If only in the beginning someone said   *i wish us both to do more than survive*
If only i began *i'm no i-   sland   peninsula maybe*   or *you & me—that's an oasis*
If cruise ship vouchers
If international time share markets   predated the middle passage
If *forever-ever* the lighthouse   unlatched   illuminating north-south
If compass doors guarded in   toward a soul &   lashed at an id: *the fuck out!*
If the British docked for democracy   offloaded ballot boxes   back in Boston
If in the beginning   said someone   *my fig peels are your tea leaves*
they'd never have to suffer   honey whiskey   industry-   mixers   general
awkwardness   at the water cooler municipal building house senate judiciary
They'd extend voting rights   to felons   sun people & immigrants   because
it's obvious   Ancient   as my neighbor next door   knocking to borrow
hot sauce   Man would rather live w/   than w/o   *& if they like fish & grits*
& all that pimp shit   they'd consider   the priceless comfort of   breath

Even in Gretna, Hearing the Cashier Talk, I Long for Gretna

after Basho

Coasting into my old world to help
mom pack up the house she can't sell
for nothing rimmed as it is with trash
and canals threatening to overflow
I get a taste for the red drink
of my youth and when the cashier
at the gas station lets slip the drawl
of my people most of them scattered
elsewhere or to the grave I could weep
peacock talk purposely showy and slow
any time I'd hit the twang mom got angry
because I was *letting my Gretna show*
she threatened a face slap or taste of soap
and I circled on a red bike just out of reach

LANDON MCGEE

Saint Paul's Chapel

Near the county line, Falls County, TX

My mother used to stop here on her way
to Waco in the summers, just to look
the chapel over. Smiling, she would say
that it reminded her of shells she took
from Alys Beach, all white and unadorned
and beautiful for being what they were.
I used to stop here too, when I was worn
out on the road but can't admit to her
that once I parked here trying to renew
a faith I'd almost given up by then,
and weeping, faced that empty field of

(you)

and knew

I'd never get it back again.

Years on,

my Lord,   you still

won't answer me.

Small grace,

this life I've made

inside the   empty.

Southern Gun Culture: A Sidebar

I'm thinking about the night my brother
intercepted Dad in his underwear
going downstairs with a loaded revolver
to dispatch the possum he imagined
was pilfering cat food in the garage,
my brother trying to reason that he
might shoot a pet or neighbor instead,
pleading with him just to go back to bed.

Dad got as far as the kitchen before
coming to his senses, emerging from
the fever dream to surrender his firearm,
slowly ascending into the same darkness
that would later reclaim him, the troubled
sleep from which we never seem to awaken.

CAROL PARRIS KRAUSS

When Summer Burns and Men Become Monsters

At night, I hear chela running along the chain link fence.
Come morning, bones and bits of fur litter the backlot.

The fairies don't frequent their ring anymore and songbirds
have abandoned the feeders as Pearl River stands stagnant.

Summer heat sheaths the city, but I know better than to open
my window, let in a gasp of air. Of late, they hunt more frequently.

Scream more often. Mercury boils. Breaks free from its glass cage.
Runs red on the kitchen linoleum. Even God's house can't withstand

the scorch. Mama twists the corner of her apron, as the pressure cooker
hisses. She wrings her hands raw. Has given up the stoop.

Neighborly chats. She added an extra lock to the back door. She
can't keep it out. I part and peer out the curtains when she isn't looking.

Tippy toes to reach the window sill. I know more than I should.
I watch, wait for it to end. Mississippi, 1964. A slow summer burn.

Fatality #9

United States Department of Labor
Mine Safety and Health Administration
Final Report of Investigation
Fatal Falling, Rolling, or Sliding Rock

Accident at Surface Facility (Cement)
Calera, Shelby County, Alabama
Mine I.D. 01-0609 Plant: Roberta
Here follows a description of the event:

Victim reported to work at 7 a.m.
Travelled to the top of a 318 foot
Vertical duct tower and rappelled in
While measuring wall thickness an object

Fell from above and struck him on the head
No one witnessed the accident—found dead

Smash

Infinitive: To bang, to hit, to pound,
to get up in the guts. Honey, I crush
on you; that is to say, I want your sound
in the parts of me that I can't see, so hush
and let me hear you breathe. To screw, to nail—
don't think I mean to do you wrong, it's just
the words at my disposal always fail
communicating elements of trust.
To rail, to fuck—see what I mean? Your hands
becoming verbs, your whole body subject—
or is it mine?—to brutal new demands,
no gentler recourse. If you object,
babe, say the word, whatever word you choose
the substitute for language we refuse.

a little bit of blackitolism revisited

Across

1. a chunky flame flickers in the spaces
2. between the fingers around it. a black
3. and mild dangling from lips has this signature
4. a bright cherry from which smoke twirls upward
5. jewels popped, wears crisp, jam not to be missed
6. sixteen akhs in soul-circle cypher
7. yo yo yo, where's da homie dat beatbox?
8. mama say she hear it in his voice array

Down

9. this brooklyn styling got the gawds smiling
10. *leflaur leflah eshkoshka*
11. meaning something like "we just wilin' out"
12. how b-boys rock the document to the break
13. where people come apart in they own ears
14. from rhymes kicked, the immutable ever

a little bit of blackitolism revisited with answers

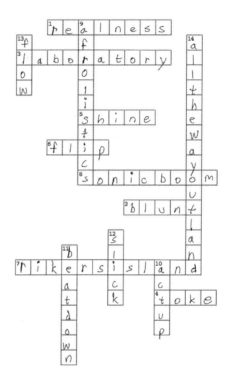

Across
1. a chunky flame flickers in the spaces
2. between the fingers around it. a black
3. and mild dangling from lips has this signature
4. a bright cherry from which smoke twirls upward
5. jewels popped, wears crisp, jam not to be missed
6. sixteen akhs in soul-circle cypher
7. yo yo yo, where's da homie dat beatbox?
8. mama say she hear it in his voice array

Down
9. this brooklyn styling got the gawds smiling
10. *leflaur leflah eshkoshka*
11. meaning something like "we just wilin' out"
12. how b-boys rock the document to the break
13. where people come apart in they own ears
14. from rhymes kicked, the immutable ever

A passing thought at the Colorado River overpass

a golden shovel after Langston Hughes' "Suicide's Note"

the gift given from another woman's womb. the
light of her reason for believing in something higher, calm.
soothes itself with food & drink & meds. cool
down from the stomached heat & maelstrom. face
the blue electric ringing throughout his circuitry of
nerves channels that yelp & bark this son sighs the
daylight away waits for night a brown river
below bridge. all this son ever asked
for was unconditional love. from his second mother. me,
myself, conditioned to loathe my flesh for
what seems like luckily half a lifetime. a
quick jump into the snowy air: flecks that kiss

(Abandoned) (Ribcage)

Record the meow of the large orange cat and measure
the length of his whiskers.

Shake the crib corners for strands of fur. Milk
stains extracted for toxicology
reports. Read them by moonlight. Paraphrase
chemical compositions in the   death
certificate. Pin it to your ribcage.
Do not read the online funeral home
messages of comfort.

                         Angels designed
from her DNA like a dinosaur
built with tadpole hearts: the universe withheld its brutal plan.

                         Do not seek answers.
Do not open your mailbox. Do not scan the sky for signs
of abandoned starlight.

Feelin' Fine

On the day the canned tarantula expires
Arguably for the second time, a meadow
Enters a poem as a transitional image
While short *i*'s, like kindergartners, line up
To go outside. The algorithm is winning
Because it is bringing you what you like,
The Matrix starring a sun-dried tomato,
A bestselling book made of worms, etc.——

there's a fever garden where you can forgive
anyone for anything, and the bodies
piling up in it are feeling fine, the dynamic
rating system they use to give feedback
has been hovering around a 4.2/5 for years:
mostly agreeable, with a few curmudgeons

Slick

after Kim Addonizio's "Winter Solstice"

I can't think about the black slick on the river or the deer
who doesn't arise from the slick of its birth, the mother
licking her fawn's wilting body. Does she hear the morning

waking around her, the red fox niggling near the den, the squeal
of the field mouse when clasped by the hawk? I can't think
about another season of slicing cold as the days shorten and leaves

slick the ground while darkness seeps across the day like another
black slick back in the Gulf after yet another storm. Catastrophe

never disappears. Pearly mussels are gone from fresh waters
of Tennessee rivers, killed by men in suits who designed the dams
to power the paper mills and chemical plants whose filth slicked

more waters. I can't think about the Tennessee pearls
gathered like shimmery tears on my mother's necklace,
now boxed in black velvet, and which I will never wear.

Sonnet II

for ricardo flores magón

I would read articles about people
placed in refrigerated trucks and I
stopped going outside to public places
no news outlets could be trusted to tell
the truth and you I couldn't stop reading
your words because you knew that the rich
are afraid the poor will seize them by the
neck and snatch their riches amassed from our hands
but in truth, we are occupied right now
avoiding gunshots in grocery stores
inside schools, at one point you too were lost
in the desert the glare of the sun
reflecting off bones while the police looked
for you too

On the Ferry to Algiers

for Lisa Pasold

You can't just sleep anywhere. There are trees. Breathe through it.
Any bright horse will do. When in doubt, pull the e-break. Then pull the second one.
All this floating, what's it for? A child holds a stuffed lamb. Throws the lamb overboard.
Algiers. The ferry drops you ass backwards. In Gibraltar. Went to see the monkeys but had
no money. Ate chips and imagined the animal calls. I don't want to leave this boat. This cargo.
Swinging hammocks. The river. Not known for its empathy. That time I was mugged in Iquitos.
Oozed and opened. Mushy scabs on my ankles. He dragged me three blocks and deposited me
on the river bank. Ran into the floating village. Scabs for months. Slept sitting up to keep from
splitting. Facing the tree line. Even the hammock caked bloody. No power on the boat. Dead
cow in the river. Five men bulged but they did it. Pushed her in. Dead car too. Ten men for that.
No dead horse but one sick one. Breathe through it. Three days of diarrhea. Told the horse to
hoof it. What's all this floating for. We drank from the river. Before the cow sunk,
she looked sleepy. Like she could
sleep anywhere.

Abstract Duality

for George Drew

Hanging strikingly
on the gray wall

of the gallery
is an oversized piece

of abstract art—
blank white

outlined in black
like a chalkboard

to be written
with meanings

about living or dying
in the deep south

or about being or nonbeing
in the floating world.

Little Louisiana Rooms

for Darrell Bourque

How can you not be pulled into the orbit
of a man who makes sonnets out of angels
in his mother's back, out of desire, dreams,
apparitions, embarkations, and ordinary light?

How can you not enjoy the company of one
who spends much of his time building rooms
constructed of syllables and slanted beams

of rhyme? How not applaud the freedom
implicit in extending an ordinary pentameter
to six- and seven-beat lines, and then some

if the exquisite room he's trying to construct
demands it, assonance and dissonance the glue
that holds it all together? How not admire
the grace to make of little rooms a mansion?

Second-Rate Mystic

for Iry LeJeune

I had everything I needed to become a second-rate mystic.
I was blind but I could read some signs & braille & weather.
I wore no shoes most of the time & I walked through thick
woods & in open prairie. In parceled light the only measure

I knew was true was measured sound. So, I made breakdowns
& two-steps & laments, easy as flowers turning to sun. I broke
the mold of who I was supposed to be with air. Newly mown

grasses were song & Caillette's lowing too. I dreamed of yokes
of love & bridges to love. Waltzes tied to the names of towns,
to branches in trees & to those cordoned off & lonely & broke,

that's how I chose to go. I spent almost all my days in an attic
no one knew, except maybe Wilma and Adeline later, tethers
I didn't even understand. My magic was never mystic magic.
Air in Lacassine is the mystic, like air moving through feathers.

Revelations

Now we will also spend a substantial portion
Of time replacing desire with solar and wind,
Though books may be ordered exercises, dictating
What kinds of work they want on the cusp, on not
Simply because of the skill for the unending future,
A self is a must, vast nations shuttered, winters
Recriminated and regretted, needless to say, placing
A set of verses on an arbitrary continuum
Is equally absurd to David or Isaiah or Paul,
Abdicating readerly duties, tentative
But subject to revision—my dear drivel,
Repent, address any bureaucratic issues,
Wordless time, a sanguine syllabus of saints,
Fixed eyes falter, a generation delivered.

Arkansas Bans Healthcare for Trans Youth

Ozark flowers coat the roadside with a quiet bloom
  of blue and violet. The yellow bursts find room
between the grasses, grab at rays of falling light.
  I look out driving home and ponder how, despite
rain and grazing deer, resilience lives, their denial
  of removal. Blossoms last till morning, bring a smile,
show me how much I need stems cracking slabs
  of concrete, springstruck life. Parked, I pick scabs
off my arm and picture our survival. How flowers
  here resemble folks so beautiful they cannot
help but dance alone in quiet rooms. Who sway
  together, knit a field nobody else can scythe.
Night swells, but we don't stop taking shafts of
  deserved sun. We hold our brilliance in dim hours.

On the First Day of the Year

The Dream is still unclaimed. The dragon fights sleep
and loses, beset by silence and the moon's fluorescent buzz.
It's been at work since it can remember; the man like smoke
said here, a pile of jewels and IOUs, you watch them.

Then he left. Of course, the terrible lizard needs to sleep—
we all do. It also needs to work, so it does that first. No discussion
of lunch breaks or shift change, and the only perks are a roasted
gold-seeker here and there—the gig gets old fast.

We all do. Four decades in retail jobs and my mother's bones sing
on the drive home, rattling in the car that won't pass next inspection,
echoing tales of heroes who just had to put the time in
and they'd be rewarded. Stories that their punch cards,

sharpened by the years, would finally bring the dragon to rest: one move
through the neck, clean like an engine turning over on the first try.

For once the engine turned over on the first try.
Oxygen humming through the steel, feeding
a fire that feeds a family, hi ho, hi ho,
it's off one job and on to another.

The gig economy is a glass of marbles.
The gig economy is pressing down on the neighborhood
and when it briefly lifts, that gap is called debt.
Enter: more marbles to fill that gap, we are

anxious when not being tamped down, pressured,
trampled. Enter: an exasperated scientist tying a series
of tubes, trying to cobble together a companion
for the human experiment, an internet of unfinished parts.

Between shifts, our phones alight with loved ones:
the years in our hands, all sing and touch.

We have gone a year without the sting of touch.
The offices of intimacy have boarded their windows,
shredded punch cards, and via a complex messaging system
of carrier pigeons and telepathy, as a collective decided

to reroute business as usual to video chat platforms.
When in the last year have I made my body a danger
to others? Unused to negative space around me
as a requirement. In a feast of empty we are overfull.

In this bright dopamine drip, this screen we touch
instead of each other, we numb ourselves to light.
I want to hold those I love like an outlet holds a plug,
electric the living amidst a glow that lets us see

face after face, in plain air, not digitized by safety, the chance
to memorize the angles of our faces, take them in our hands.

Saudade

Not so much the cold gets in, but the heat
goes out of this ramshackle house. I know
that much but don't believe it. And belief
won't keep the cold out and won't plug the leaks.
I've installed storm windows and stuffed rags
in door cracks. I let morning light shine
through east-facing windows and shutter them
at night—commonsense things. Still, cold leaks in.
A neap tide of loss drawn high by the moon
and vacuum you left seeps through the floorboards,
pools in the corners, and laps up the stairs,
until I retreat to the wreck of your room
and wonder—the closest I come to prayer—
are you warm out there, beyond the world's rim?

CHRISTIAN J. COLLIER

Nothing Glowed

after we shed our clothes atop the black boulder & leapt

after we became half-moons in the summer air before finding water

after our naked skin fed the creek

after the rain came quiet intruding

you begged the saints between the drops to listen to us what hymns they heard

what slow gospel as your mouth branded my inner thigh again & again

we needed a new anthem we made one from one another

i went under the spell of your pierced tongue its chorus making me forget briefly

the verdict the world stripped from us earlier ██████ got away with killing

on the other end of that gutting

an exhaustion

in our ruddy cells

we wished to be strangers to   another death

before our deaths

47

Sonnet for the armadillo in the front yard

an armadillo rolls up as the rent raises our hedges
asked who here holds a candle to the moon
the streetlight flicking like a landlord's wrist
outside the complex, no eviction notice

came so far to fawn where the woods cut down
just like a bad joke somebody took to heart
the facebook posted fence—pornos for privacy,
an armored car on loop looking for food

to size up spotted baby on the byway
side of the town who holds a vigil's root
word for the vigilant: we will protect
ourselves from property else one another

protect us from ourselves. no god will know
who holds the keys but who will sing

BENJAMIN MORRIS

Old Highway 80 (to Meridian)

With luck, you'll never see me again.
Diverted not once but twice—first from your day
then again from the route you planned to take
you reach for the map, as if my thin
black ribbon could be unwound. But no.
Unlike my younger brother, who drapes across
this state like a belt, all I own is loss:
my length, cut like a root when the hoe
bites down; my woods, cleared for either concrete
or graves; even my one last town is named
Lost Gap. Behold its cabin hollowed by flame
and be grateful, friend, that as soon as we meet
we depart. But ask yourself before you go—
you don't really believe in luck—do you?

Argelès-sur-Mer

Tourist town, all families and umbrellas, sunscreen
and cheap motels. The code sent to my phone, releasing

the hotel key from a machine on the wall, no front desk.
Our friend's mother, raised in Lyon, came here as a child,

recommended the stop. Early July heat. The Mediterranean's
humidity like trips to the Gulf when I was young. In the market

we eat sticky crepes, take pictures of stacked fruit and hand-knotted
rugs. Love, will we always be childless? Sitting on the porch

of our rented room, drinking champagne from plastic cups that came
wrapped in plastic, I think, *I couldn't add anything to this.*

You go for a swim, and I watch you wading through the waves
while I sit on the beach with our things—your glasses,

the book I brought but never started. My heels make little craters.
A boy packs a bucket full of sand, turns it over to make a house.

for luck: an Arkansas Sonnet

There is no new weather here / so close to the well of being
wasp in the lampstand tick in the beard / moon visible day and night
but I'm grateful for azaleas / coming back grateful for muck boots
for folks who fix things / for hummingbirds' full feeders
and dead carpenter ants / for gardens and hoes and summer
tomatoes above all grateful for / walking the train tracks
with two new pennies / you and me looking for luck.

I.   My football team is winning

and my granddaddy's still dead. He swats
an almighty yellowjacket from a star-soaked
can of Coke while our tailgate moves farther
out on the asphalt grid. We've got a healthy
lead. We've got a blond quarterback with eyes
like the last two red salmon pouting pink face
to face in a river that forgot rock,
forgot North. When I couldn't read the score

they gave me glasses, and the grit smoothed in
to smother. When the blond drops back to pass
his footwork blesses deviled eggs, cold ham.
If he slings an interception, settle
in, belt out a rag. If my granddaddy's
an angel, blow the whistle, throw the flag.

II.   My football team is winning

so I carry my first-born son by feet
And hands up the mountain. He shivers
in November sun like wheat, gold
and clean for threshing. No ram bucks
in the thicket. He hears no sound,
his first touchdown a trick after they stop us
on third and one. Coach's son holds
for the kicker, draws it up and rolls
to his left to connect with another son,
sons pile the end zone, sons slap
the helmets of sons of sons, sons in stands
drone as the defense lines up again. All of us
here to worship. All of us here to burn.

Before Moving to Austin

You should know this city's thirst for copper-
tinged sediment & meat fresh from the workers
of the dying farms & fields—is never sated.
The most American thing we've done: let them in
through the back door & give them a uniform to die in.
No one wants to admit this city, sick without a steady flux
of salt-leaking bodies, will turn in on itself & chew
on my sisters. Their faces, an edible bouquet
of Black & Brown & bloody balloons; my brothers, their ghosts
hanging like spinach in the city's teeth, swing
from construction cranes as flags for the dead
or dying. You should know—this city
would eat its young
for a profit.

Pain Psalm

Under   the skin   under the silver   fascia
over the living bone   its honeycomb   around
its secret knitting   clothing the marrow   through
and through   the viscera   the redblack   darkness
there   a lightning-struck tree   a flash   of writhing
In the midnight   of the body   pain   At noon
though visible   to no man   or machine   pain
What is born   and borne   no language   touches
You promised   no more   than we could   bear
Where is the healer   or the hound   who can chase it
What gunshot   can scatter   the gnawing   beasts
If no healer   no Catahoula   bitch   to bay
no bullet   or snare   to unseize   this body   You made
Then God   I am left to beg: un-sic Yourself   from me

Semi-Automatic Sonnet

Raccoon is curled by curb, its blood the shape
of half the moon beside it. Coyote
is splayed with jaw an opening, a gate
through which the insects glitter, canid teeth,

hard candy of maggots, gleam in headlights
the air is thick with flies, the shoulder flush
with mother deer, who bloat before the flight
of crows arrive for organs. These will lush

the field behind the road when vultures drop
them. Don't mind the mother toad or the brood
of fresh cicadas trilling *what a false
and fickle life. Don't mind*, they say, *shooting*

will test your constitution, violence cries,
no reasons left to keep its child alive.

T. R. HUMMER

Stranger

The black rhino is not, how people say here, my *intimate*.
The Bengal tiger does not curl next to me cold nights
Grooming its tail with an inhuman tongue. The lowland gorilla
Looks like family but would tear off my arm at the scapula
And use it to smash my skull. The world is dying, pigeon
By auroch by skink by ibex, though the Amazon
Pink river dolphin is your daughter's spirit animal.
Who no longer laughs even near you? The laughing owl.
If I translate for you *My sister is dying, my friend is dying*,
Everything you're doing will just go on—what's the word?—
Forever. And that is, like the vanishing of some obscure bird,
Perfectly normal, for we don't stop being, do we, flying
Off the terminal earth like damselflies just because strangers go.
Turn and live, camerado. Is there anyone here you don't know?

AURIELLE MARIE

sonnet while ziptied in a police wagon, fulton county

i have my suspicions: no one watches over sparrows. in my mother's eyes
there's only he who listens to me blaspheme. i boast the truth about my
own magic, goad my mother's jealous god with prayers sharpened like knives.
i kneel for the cool pleasure: i know my mother's god like a lover. she swears
i'll be caught by the hook of a noose, realize the power of her disastrous
god. but 13 died in a chapel while praising *the great listener.* what glory.
a 13-year-old killed during bedtime prayer just yesterday, her hands pressed
to her chest. and i assume she called just before, upon a righteous god, fallen silent. then bullet.
we sat in paddy wagons after that, sure of our deaths. with my hands tied to my feet,
my feet shackled to the floor. defiant as a scorned lover, i sing. my mother prays *but to who?*
my voice breaks, my mouth a god of sound. tired of beating me, the police, they laughed.
my mother's god fit in my pocket. waited until the coast was cleared to show his face. the first sounds
he chewed into a word—*Sorry.* & I am too, you God of Ruin.

God of Dead Children, and the Police.

AURIELLE MARIE

Unsonnet for the Poems So Black They Are Misread

it's July & the heat rises from the middle of the ghetto

   & no one leaves home unless they have a death wish

   & my mother does. pulled a butcher's knife from beneath her pillow

   & snuck into the neighbor's yard, kills the dog and steals us gourdfruit

   & for her children she cubes a feast she could not afford

   & like so many of my wounds, she sliced them brilliantly, my mother

      & a warrior

      & suicidal

      & gave me a memory for that summer, one red

      & unwelcomed

        & in case she needed to leave us, left us this.

        & i guess here: I love my mama. I cut her into triangles and chew

          & I'm a tree of watermelon. My mama's only daughter. fruit between her teeth.

      & that's the poem.

Baby care instructions

Before you lived, I lived inside my own
loathing. Some parents have children to replace
themselves, but we're two instead of none.
Pushing you on a swing, sunset, my hands
on your mammalian back, I remember
how everyone thought I'd kill you by mistake,
my throat in hives because I believed
them. You made me, too, daughter drawing
the last sip from a juicebox, wisps of hair
rising in the dirty breeze. I show you
how to kick to propel yourself, and all threat
dips like the sun behind the jungle gym.
I may have been born a knife, but my daughter
won't be a knife, nor its willing sheath.

Prayer Shawl

The work of a prayer shawl is to love
the weight it holds, the blue yarns heavy
with the ache of shoulders, of cold like winter rain,
the gray yarns grave as tears. A voice struggles
to rise from the wool, but the cry fails and falls
and the hurt breast is unconsoled.

But the Galilee ladies who gather on Sundays
to knit their prayers into a woman's fear
and hug her prayers into theirs, know
that in the diamond honeycomb stitch,
or the hurdle and purl ridge stitches,
hope turns and casts on the heart's fibers
and the ladies believe, needles flashing.

How to Locate a Homeless Daughter

Search for vocal warmups and tongue twisters,
repeat, *the big black bug drank black blood*.
Be the big black bug that drank black blood,
antennae and tiny hairs tuned to Missouri
Case.net, six legs cycling through
litigant name searches and jail rosters.
Flail pincers when you find her caged, rest
briefly knowing she can eat and can't use.
With compound eyes see all her anguished
faces—realize you're wingless and in this
moment your exoskeleton fractured.
Say, *bug crawled upon the balcony*
in explicitly imitating her hiccupping,
while aimlessly inviting her in.

GEORGE DAVID CLARK

Washing Your Feet

Stranger, they are dirty. You've come so far
so harshly: bloody miles through silt and brambles,
noxious bogs and mud-fields, dunes of char
beneath the sun-spill—all of it in sandals.
Please take my chair; this dry, blond Scotch on ice
will douse your pride. I kneel to yawn the straps
that bite your ankles, loose the vamps that vise
your tarsals, slide bruised heels into my lap.
There's fragrant water in the wooden vessel,
sanded smooth and gauged so that your stride
can lose its travel in the lather's pestle
and cascade. You're no one, and you're special,
drawn to leave before you're even dried,
the paths bathed off revealing paths inside.

hoppinjohn: a blues

after Tyehimba Jess

she's got some eyes—bette davis, no, black—
on our plates, she shimmies between the rice
and makes a lucky meal where there is lack—
not lima, pinto, just blackeyes suffice.

what alchemy where peas become pennies,
where even here we can be rich with pork,
this meal is tender medicine, ready
to heal what keeps us broken, to unyoke

ourselves away from helpless and enslaved.
we slice we sear we simmer and we braise
we hunt we chop we pick we stand amazed,
we serve it up and then we offer praise

blackeyed peas and
we pray this meal

the white blending around it—a whole note
supple with salt and onion and butter
this marriage on our Sunday plate, we float—
this here's a john that hops like no other.

the currency we want is born of soil,
stewed and heaped while the crops break for winter.
when we need fresh warm hope, brought to the boil,
so we're not chained to ruin, we splinter

and we build ourselves a future, we cook
it down until it's soft enough to eat,
we count our blessings, count the faith it took
to be here, to have vegetables and meat.

white rice on new year's day,
will keep the doom away—

Come Fool Circle: A Three-Poem Cycle of Fourteen-Word Sonnets

(1)	(2)	(3)
Paris	So,	Because
being	if	when
Paris	what	I
doesn't	goes	write
change	up	what
the	*must*	I
fact	come	know,
the	down,	once
Eiffel	then	upon
Tower's	falling	a
still	isn't	time
in	failing . . .	*is*
someone's	it's	the
backyard.	flying.	end.

SAMUEL PRESTRIDGE

Sonnet with Cheese, No Mayo:
At a Burger Joint Drive-Thru, I Remember a Rookie Calf, Running & Kicking & Being a Dick

I saw, driving home from work, a pasture
on the right. I saw among the placid,
grazing herd, anomalous, a manic
calf, not two ticks older than yesterday,

start up from wary, experimental
grazing and, at a broken-field run, kick
at air, kick sideways at the principle
of standing still again. God bless his slick,

pristine ignorance of a future writ
in hamburger, how his fluttering hooves
will fuel creeping toward the take-out window
and measuring my life by car lengths moved.

While offering him our requiescat,
I tell the server *No.*

No fries with that.

Texan Sonnet for a Historic Freeze

I should step outside, lose myself in the
snow-covered parking lot, walk to
the grocery store across the street and
keep walking, my fog of breath proof
I'm alive. It is the first Ash Wednesday
I have an excuse for not kneeling in a pew,
but my mortality is still in the room
with me. My water comes and goes.
Mostly goes. Others have it worse.
What choices do I have? Do I water my cat
or make more pasta during rare moments
of power? Do I leave the land of state violence
in the name of Christ? Or stay and destroy
myself. The doorknob is frozen shut.

Letter to the Man Possessed by Demons

Night and day among the tombs and in the hills
he would cry out and cut himself with stones.
                                    —Mark 5:5

I thought Christ was the spoon
    that hollows the gourd, the fist

pulling out that stringy seed,
    but he only made an opening:

I had to see myself through it.
    You don't have to tell me how

you went back and buried all
    the drowned swine, I know.

I'm like you: a lover of graves
    and the dirt it takes to fill them.

Don't be ashamed. If you come here,
    we won't talk about that

other life. I will prepare a meal,
    you will tell me your new name.

But Where To from Here?

(an almost sonnet, for the almost forgotten)

into our nomadic earlobes, idiot
noise: a drumming the heart creates—
  when it returns demanding jpegs
of flashback, raw—complete with audio

  shapeshifting alongside time, in which
change is an elusive chameleon,
  as if history can't be repeated
but it can: see—unable to flee

  we had been landlocked by bodies, ours—
thinking about a lil' song, no rhyme,
  invisible thematic threads between
the language of cartography, igniting

  that flicka-flame of *i want you*, we were
danger crisscrossing into disastrous.
  tell me—when memory regurgitates
relic ghost once believed eradicated,

  do we love the paranormal image
.or. outrun a past   without a future?

MAGGIE GRABER

From "southeastern crown"

grey dust :: grey mask of moon :: up :: grey moon :: her
+ a line of stars :: each night :: orion
hunts the wild sky :: the greeks :: speak :: seven
sisters :: pleiades :: what is the word for
forever :: it must be :: queer :: must be sky
without end :: the forest :: millennia
of rock :: mycelial :: soil :: plenty
where that came from :: creek bed sand :: firefly ::
the moon a grey circle :: i am naked
+ freckled as night :: listen :: fire snaps
its orange hands + i become its loyal
subject :: it burns through dead :: basic
as air :: i dig my heels in cold sand ::
a mountain :: we hold each pose :: like a howl ::

On Alternate Endings

In one end of *The Butterfly Effect*,
Ashton Kutcher's character returns to
    his own birth, takes the umbilical cord
and strangles himself. The message being

    some evil necessitates such extremes.
But other endings proved it possible
    to rid the world of that evil without
resorting to such a thing. There are ways

    to have your cake and lose it, too. I once
dreamt every night of a veranda I
    never knew, thirteen and so lonely—
a veranda where my mother appeared,

    my baby sister wrapped in her arms. *Look*,
she'd say. *She's here. She's been here all along.*

CODY SMITH

Sonnet Beginning with Lines from Keats and Ending in Dust

When I have fears my name will live beyond
    this flesh that years will pull to vellum,
  I know yet still my children, then grown
    thick and hunkering in their late days, will read
about a son, about a daughter I held
    in these hands which they had yet let go,
  these hands like my father's saddle, broken,
    hanging from a joist in a barn only touched
by a horse-hair braided breeze heavy with hay dust,
    and I think even dew sliding from the dark
  bracken returns again even if we don't notice it,
    even if we don't care, the dust of my bones,
dust of my voice, dust on my name on a book spine
    on a shelf waiting for you, my loves.

You're Not a Bee

ARDOT PSA Message

Two stone white cranes
flying over a drainage ditch
in love not with each other
but with the idea of being birds
born for some other world
and placed here for a purpose
beyond their knowing. Here on
a road you've traveled
a hundred times is a church
in a cloud of harvested grain
you've never seen before.
Up ahead there's a cardboard box
lifting up into the air from
the back of a pickup truck.

At the Audubon Exhibit in Auburn, Alabama, the Still-Weeping Mother of God

I imagine the scarlet rosefinch earned
her name only after the pins were placed,
pink specimen small enough to needle
to a board meant for moths. The plaque silvering
the glass edge of her tomb says she was runted,
too tiny to hope for a long life, but—
that's not true, is it? Look at her: wings spread
like the graceful arms of a martyr,
the slightest turn to her lowered head, closed
eyes downcast, a Pietà in blush, no
godchild lying dead across her lap but
what he represents still there in the hollow
of her breast: a heart snuffed out. Look at her
face, her sadness, the blood: She lived.

Birmingham Double Sonnet

Sunset at Railroad Park and the city
is baring its teeth: overpass and oak
the jagged jawbones of carnivores, black
against red sky, skyscrapers silvery
windows throwing back shadow and light.
Cranes stretching their long necks to heaven,
this place always building, going up.
I walk with Jake around what was once
a viaduct, symbol of progress, now
collapsed into a man-made lake, and
the city begins to glow from within,
a man-made heart, a buzzing nerve.
He tells me he keeps trying to leave
but it won't stick, Birmingham's canines

biting his coattails like a starved dog
scenting a scrap of food. It's violent—
this animal, its long-throated
history, insatiable gut. But Jake isn't
bitter; he lets the city swallow him
whole. He says he's been hungry before,
knows what good a little food, some small
show of kindness, can do. Besides—
we were children here. This is where we learned
that a place can break your heart from outside
and within, street names and skylines sweet
and bitter in the blood, no outrunning
what built you even when it leaves a bruise.
We were always meant to come home.

Acknowledgments

The following poems first appeared in other publications:

Rasha Abdulhadi, "Counterpoint to an Insect Collection," *Mizna.*

Stacey Balkun, "Carthage," *The Sonnets Anthology* (Hermeneutic Chaos Press, 2016).

Anna Lena Phillips Bell, "August, Nantahala National Forest," *Hampden-Sydney Poetry Review.*

Andrea Blancas Beltran, "Border Sonnet: Special Census of the Population of El Paso, Tex. January 15, 1916," *Borderlands: Texas Poetry Review.*

Darrell Bourque, "Second-Rate Mystic," *Where I Waited* (Yellow Flag Press, 2016).

Wendy Taylor Carlisle, "for luck: an Arkansas Sonnet," *ONE ART.*

George David Clark, "Washing Your Feet," *Ecotone.*

Dorsey Craft, "I: My football team is winning," *Boudin: The McNeese Review Online.*

Hannah Dow, "My Mother Tries to Teach Me How to Pray," *Nimrod International Journal.* "My Mother Tries to Teach Me about Language," *EcoTheo Review.*

CD Eskilson, "Arkansas Bans Healthcare for Trans Youth," *New Delta Review.*

David Greenspan, "Now is what has happened," *Soundings East.*

Raye Hendrix, "Birmingham Double Sonnet" as "Coming Home," *Poetry Birmingham Literary Journal* (UK).

Maggie Rue Hess, "A Sonnet, Because I Didn't Want to Say, 'I Already Knew,'" *GASHER*.

Faylita Hicks, "Before Moving to Austin," *F(r)iction*.

Erin Hoover, "Baby care instructions," *Shenandoah* and included in *No Spare People* (Black Lawrence Press, forthcoming, Fall 2023).

SG Huerta, as "A Semi Sonnet for a Texas Snowstorm," *FERAL: A Journal of Poetry and Art*.

Jules Jacob, "How to Locate a Homeless Daughter," included in *Kingdom of Glass & Seed* (Lily Poetry Review Books, forthcoming, Fall 2023).

Edison Jennings, "Saudade," *Valparaiso Poetry Review*.

Ashley M. Jones, "hoppinjohn: a blues," *Oxford American*.

Aurielle Marie, "sonnet while ziptied in a police wagon, fulton county" as "unholy ghazal," *The Adroit Journal*.

Caleb Nolen, "Letter to the Man Possessed by Demons," *Shenandoah*.

Alison Pelegrin, "Even in Gretna, Hearing the Cashier Talk, I Long for Gretna," *Our Lady of Bewilderment* (LSU Press, 2022), reprinted with permission.

Samuel Prestridge, as "4/5th a Sonnet," *Better than Starbucks*.

Suzanne Underwood Rhodes, "Prayer Shawl," © *Christian Century,* reprinted with permission, January 2023 issue.

Tom Snarsky, "Feelin' Fine," *Reclaimed Water* (Ornithopter Press, 2023), reprinted with permission.

Jim Whiteside, "Argelès-sur-Mer," *fourteen poems* (UK).

Marcus Wicker, "First Contact: ATLien Observes Love," *32 Poems.* "ATLien Considers Neighborliness as a Conditional Concept," *BOMB Magazine.*

Marianne Worthington, "Slick," *Thimble Literary Magazine.*

Contributors

RASHA ABDULHADI (Mountain South): *who is owed spring-time* (Neon Hemlock, 2021). Work in *Snaring New Suns, Unfettered Hexes, Halal if You Hear Me.*

BRANDON AMICO (Western NC): *Disappearing, Inc.* (Gold Wake Press, 2019). Work in *Best American Poetry 2020, Kenyon Review, North American Review, Southern Humanities Review.*

JC ANDREWS (Springfield, AR): Work in/forthcoming in *New Ohio Review, The Massachusetts Review, Gulf Coast.*

SUSAN APRIL (Myersville, MD): *French Class* (Loom Press, 1999). Work in/forthcoming in *The Lowell Review, Heron Tree, Collateral.*

STACEY BALKUN (New Orleans, LA): *Sweetbitter* (Sundress Publications, 2022), *Jackalope-Girl Learns to Speak* (dancing girl press, 2016); editor of *Fiolet & Wing: An Anthology of Domestic Fabulist Poetry* (Liminal Books, 2019).

MAKALANI BANDELE (Louisville, KY): *(joppappy and the sentence-makers are) eponymous as funk* (Futurepoem, forthcoming), *under the aegis of a winged mind* (Autumn House Press, 2020), *hell-fightin'* (Willow Books, 2011). Work in/forthcoming in *Obsidian, Washington Square Review, Sou'wester.*

ANNA LENA PHILLIPS BELL (Coast of what's now called North Carolina): *Smaller Songs* (St Brigid Press, 2020), *Ornament* (UNT Press, 2017). Work in *The Southern Review*, *Poetry Northwest*, *Electric Literature*.

ANDREA BLANCAS BELTRAN (El Paso, TX): Work in/forthcoming in *Tupelo Quarterly*, *Poetry Northwest*, *The Offing*.

ELLIE BLACK (Oxford, MS): Work in *Hayden's Ferry Review*, *Poet Lore*, *Mississippi Review*, *The Offing*, *Black Warrior Review*.

DARRELL BOURQUE (Rural Southwest LA): *Until We Talk* (Etruscan Press, forthcoming, Fall 2023), *migraré* (University of Louisiana Press, 2019), *Megan's Guitar and Other Poems from Acadie* (University of Louisiana Press, 2013), *In Ordinary Light: New and Selected Poems* (University of Louisiana Press, 2010).

WENDY TAYLOR CARLISLE (Arkansas Ozarks): *Reading Berryman to the Dog* (Belle Point Press, reissue 2023), *The Mercy of Traffic* (Unlikely Books, 2019); featured in *Wild Muse: Ozarks Nature Poetry* (Cornerpost Press, 2022). Work in *Rattle*, *Atlanta Review*, *Unlikely Stories*.

JUSTIN CARTER (Des Moines, IA): *Brazos* (Belle Point Press, forthcoming). Work in/forthcoming in *Bat City Review*, *Sonora Review*, *South Carolina Review*.

MICHELLE CASTLEBERRY (Watkinsville, GA): *Dissecting the Angel and Other Poems* (Miglior Press, 2013). Work in *Still: The Journal, EcoTheo Review, The Atlanta Review*.

GEORGE DAVID CLARK (McMurray, PA): *Newly Not Eternal* (LSU Press, forthcoming), *Reveille* (University of Arkansas Press, 2015).

ADAM CLAY (Hattiesburg, MS): *Circle Back* (Milkweed Editions, forthcoming), *To Make Room for the Sea* (Milkweed Editions, 2020).

CHRISTIAN J. COLLIER (Chattanooga, TN): *Greater Ghost* (Four Way Books, forthcoming), *The Gleaming of the Blade* (Bull City Press, 2022).

DORSEY CRAFT (Jacksonville, FL): *Plunder* (Bauhan Publishing, 2020). Work in/forthcoming in *Blackbird, Copper Nickel, Pleiades, Poetry Northwest*.

BRODY PARRISH CRAIG (Fayetteville, AR): *The Patient is an Unreliable Historian* (Omnidawn, forthcoming), *Boyish* (Omnidawn, 2021). Work in/forthcoming in *Poetry, Mississippi Review, Muzzle Magazine*.

HANNAH DOW (Bentonville, AR): *Rosarium* (Acre Books, 2018). Work in *Shenandoah, Image, The Southern Review*.

GEORGE DREW (Poestenkill, NY): *Just Like Oz* (Madville Publishing, 2022), *Hog: A Delta Memoir* (Bass Clef Books, 2022), *Drumming Armageddon* (Madville Publishing, 2020), *Fancy's Orphan* (Tiger Bark Press, 2017), *Pastoral Habits: New & Selected Poems* (Texas Review Press, 2016).

CD ESKILSON (Fayetteville, AR): Work in *The Offing*, *Florida Review*, *Pleiades*, *Washington Square Review*.

ANN FISHER-WIRTH (Oxford, MS): *Paradise Is Jagged* (Terrapin Books, 2023), *The Bones of Winter Birds* (Terrapin Books, 2019), *Mississippi* (with Maude Schuyler Clay; Wings Press, 2018); *The Ecopoetry Anthology* (co-edited with Laura-Gray Street, Trinity UP, 2013; 3rd printing 2020).

BETH GORDON (Asheville, NC): *How to Keep Things Alive* (Split Rock Press, forthcoming), *The Water Cycle* (Variant Literature, 2022), *This Small Machine of Prayer* (Kelsay Books, 2021).

MAGGIE GRABER (Oxford, MS): *Swan Hammer* (Michigan State University Press, 2022). Work in/forthcoming in *The Journal*, *The Louisville Review*, *Southern Indiana Review*, *Nashville Review*.

DAVID GREENSPAN (Hattiesburg, MS): *One Person Holds So Much Silence* (Driftwood Press, 2022), *Nervous System with Dramamine* (The Offending Adam, 2022). Work in *Fence*, *Narrative*, *Denver Quarterly*.

ANDREW HEMMERT (Denver, CO): *Blessing the Exoskeleton* (University of Pittsburgh Press, 2022), *Sawgrass Sky* (Texas Review Press, 2021).

RAYE HENDRIX (Eugene, OR): *What Good Is Heaven* (Texas Review Press, forthcoming). Work in *American Poetry Review, 32 Poems, Poetry Northwest.*

MAGGIE RUE HESS (Knoxville, TN): *The Bones That Map Us* (Belle Point Press, forthcoming). Work in/forthcoming in *Rattle, Connecticut River Review, The Bayou Review, Yearling.*

FAYLITA HICKS (Chicago, IL): *A Map of My Want* (Haymarket Books, forthcoming, 2024), *Hoodwitch* (Acre Books, 2019). Work in *American Poetry Review,* Academy of American Poets' *Poem-A-Day, Poetry.*

ERIN HOOVER (Middle TN): *No Spare People* (Black Lawrence, forthcoming, Fall 2023), *Barnburner* (Elixir, 2018).

RANDALL HORTON (New Jersey): *Dead Weight: A Memoir in Essays* (Northwestern UP, 2022).

SG HUERTA (Central TX): *Last Stop* (Defunkt Magazine, 2023), *The Things We Bring with Us* (Headmistress Press, 2021). Work in *The Offing, Split Lip Magazine, Infrarrealista Review.*

T.R. HUMMER (Hudson Valley, NY): *It's Not Personal* (Press 53 Silver Concho Series, forthcoming), *After The Afterlife* (Acre Books, 2019), *Eon* (LSU Press, 2018), and others.

JULES JACOB (Springfield, MO): *Kingdom of Glass & Seed* (Lily Poetry Review Books, forthcoming, Fall 2023), *Rappaccini's Garden* (co-author with Sonja Johanson, White Stag Publishing, 2023), *The Glass Sponge* (Finishing Line Press, 2013). Work in/forthcoming in *Rust + Moth*, *Westchester Review*, *Lily Poetry Review*, *Plume Poetry*.

BETHANY JARMUL (Pittsburgh, PA): *Take Me Home* (Belle Point Press, forthcoming). Work in/forthcoming in *Salamander*, *The Citron Review*, *Emerge Journal*, *Gone Lawn*, and *Cease, Cows*.

GRANT MATTHEW JENKINS (Tulsa, OK): *Contingencies of the Bourgeoisie* (BlazeVOX [books], 2023), *Ivory Tower* (novel: Atmosphere Press, 2020). Work in *Sprung Formal*, *The Laurel Review*.

EDISON JENNINGS (Abingdon, VA): *Intentional Fallacies* (Broadstone Books, 2021), *Reckoning* (Jacar Press, 2013).

ASHLEY M. JONES (Birmingham, AL): *Reparations Now!* (Hub City Press, 2021), *Magic City Gospel* (Hub City Press, 2017); *What Things Cost: an anthology for the people* (co-edited with Rebecca Gayle Howell and Emily J. Jalloul, University Press of Kentucky, 2023). Work in *Southern Living*, *Hammer & Hope*.

CAROL PARRIS KRAUSS (Portsmouth, VA): Work in/forthcoming in *ONE ART*, *Schuylkill Valley Journal*, *Story South*, *Dead Mule School of Southern Literature*, *Louisiana Literature*.

T.K. LEE (Columbus, MS): Work in *Deep South Magazine* (short fiction), *Screen Door Review* (poetry), *Jook Productions* (drama); featured in *Southern Literary Review* for *Scapegoat* (Unsolicited Press, 2022).

STEVEN LEYVA (Baltimore, MD): *The Understudy's Handbook* (Washington Writers' Publishing House, 2020). Work in *Best American Poetry 2020*, *The Common*, *The Hopkins Review*.

AURIELLE MARIE (Atlanta, GA): *Gumbo Ya Ya* (University of Pittsburgh Press, 2021). Work in Academy of American Poets' *Poem-A-Day*, *American Poetry Review*, *Poetry*, *The Slowdown*.

LANDON MCGEE (Fayetteville, AR): Work in *Bayou*, *EcoTheo Review*.

BENJAMIN MORRIS (New Orleans, LA): *Ecotone* (poetry, Antenna, 2017), *Hattiesburg, Mississippi* (nonfiction, Arcadia, 2014). Work in *The Southern Review*, *Lit Hub*, *Oxford American*, *Los Angeles Review of Books*.

CALEB NOLEN (Staunton, VA): Work in *32 Poems*, *Bat City Review*, *Image*, *The Georgia Review*.

MÓNICA TERESA ORTIZ (Lubbock, TX): *have you ever dreamed of flamingos?* (Garden Party Collective/Astringent Press, forthcoming, Fall 2023). Work in *The Brooklyn Rail*, *Scalawag*.

ALISON PELEGRIN (Covington, LA): *Our Lady of Bewilderment* (LSU Press, 2022), *Waterlines* (LSU Press, 2016).

SAMUEL PRESTRIDGE (Athens, GA): Work in *Arkansas Review*, *Literary Imagination*, *Southern Humanities Review*, *Radar*.

SUZANNE UNDERWOOD RHODES (Fayetteville, AR): *Flying Yellow: New and Selected Poems* (Paraclete Press, 2021), *Hungry Foxes* (Aldrich Press, 2013). Work in *Green Mountains Review* (American Poet Laureate Series), *Christian Century, Mid/South Anthology* (Belle Point Press, 2022).

CELESTE SCHUELER (Seattle, WA): Work in *FERAL: A Journal of Poetry and Art*, *Stone Circle Review*.

GERRY SLOAN (Fayetteville, AR): Work in *Arkansas Review*, *Cold Mountain Review*, *The Midwest Quarterly*. Featured in *Wild Muse: Ozarks Nature Poetry* (Cornerpost Press, 2022).

CODY SMITH (Montverde, FL): *Gulf* (Texas Review Press, 2019). Work in/forthcoming in *Poetry, Prairie Schooner, Mississippi Review*.

TOM SNARSKY (Northwestern VA): *Reclaimed Water* (Ornithopter Press, 2023), *Complete Sentences* (Broken Sleep Books, 2022), *Light-Up Swan* (Ornithopter Press, 2021), *Threshold* (Another New Calligraphy, 2018).

NATHAN SPOON (Nashville, TN): *The Importance of Being Feeble-Minded* (Nine Mile Books' Propel Disability Poetry Series, forthcoming). Work in *American Poetry Review, Poetry, swamp pink*.

COLIN JAMES STURDEVANT (Houston, TX): *The Rorschach Exchange* (Pondicherry Books, forthcoming). Work in/forthcoming in *Bluestem, Crab Creek Review, The Bayou Review*.

HIBA TAHIR (Fayetteville, AR): Work in/forthcoming in *Grist, Hobart After Dark, Hooligan Magazine, Zone 3, New South*.

NIKKI UMMEL (New Orleans, LA): *Bayou Sonata* (NOLA DNA, 2023), *Hush* (Belle Point Press, 2022). Work in/forthcoming in *Painted Bride Quarterly, The Adroit Journal, The Georgia Review*.

DAMIEN URIAH (Oklahoma Ozarks): Work in/forthcoming in *Cimarron Review, Thrush, Hawaii Pacific Review, About Place Journal*.

CLARA BUSH VADALA (Van Alstyne, TX): *Book of Altars* (Belle Point Press, forthcoming), *Resembling a wild animal* (ELJ Editions, forthcoming). Work in/forthcoming in *New South, The Madrigal, Moss Puppy*.

JOHN VANDERSLICE (Conway, AR): *Nous Nous* (Braddock Avenue Books, 2021), *The Last Days of Oscar Wilde* (Burlesque Press, 2018). Work in *Southern Humanities Review*, *Crazyhorse*, *Sou'wester*.

CASSANDRA WHITAKER (Onley, VA): Work in/forthcoming in *The Bennington Review*, *New South*, *Mississippi Review*.

JIM WHITESIDE (Brooklyn, NY): *Writing Your Name on the Glass* (Bull City Press, 2019). Work in *The New York Times*, *Poetry*, *American Poetry Review*, *Ploughshares*, *The Southern Review*.

MARCUS WICKER (Memphis, TN): *Silencer* (Houghton Mifflin Harcourt, 2017), *Maybe the Saddest Thing* (Harper Perennial, 2012). Work in *The Nation*, *The Atlantic*, *The New Republic*, *Oxford American*, *Poetry*.

MATTHEW WIMBERLEY (Beech Mountain, NC): *Daniel Boone's Window* (LSU Press, 2021), *All the Great Territories* (SIU Press, 2020).

MARIANNE WORTHINGTON (Southeastern KY): *The Girl Singer* (University Press of Kentucky, 2021). Work in/forthcoming in *Oxford American*, *Shenandoah*, *Calyx*, *Cheap Pop*, *Zone 3*.

JIANQING ZHENG (Itta Bena, MS): *The Dog Years of Reeducation* (Madville Publishing, 2023), *A Way of Looking* (Silverfish Review Press, 2021).

About the Editors

CASIE DODD lives in Arkansas with her husband and two children. Recent work has appeared in *The Windhover*, *Oxford American*, *Image*, *Arkansas Review*, and other journals. Based in Fort Smith, she is the founder and publisher of Belle Point Press.

C. T. SALAZAR is a Latinx poet and librarian from Mississippi. His debut collection, *Headless John the Baptist Hitchhiking*, is now available from Acre Books. He's the author of three chapbooks, most recently *American Cavewall Sonnets* (Bull City Press, 2021). He's the 2020 recipient of the Mississippi Institute of Arts and Letters award in poetry. His poems have appeared in *The Rumpus*, *Beloit Poetry Journal*, *Cincinnati Review*, *32 Poems*, *RHINO*, and elsewhere.

Belle Point Press is a regional small press based in Fort Smith, Arkansas. Our mission is to celebrate the literary culture and community of the American Mid-South: all its paradoxes and contradictions, all the ways it gets us home.

This is the second anthology by Belle Point Press. Learn more about our work at www.bellepointpress.com.

* * *

Mid/South Sonnets brings together sixty-six poets with ties throughout the American South. From Oklahoma to Florida—with larger clusters of work from the more centrally located Mid-Southern states, Arkansas, Mississippi, and Tennessee—the states represented through these writers offer a wide range of landscapes and perspectives that speak to the region's eclectic nature. While this anthology includes many conventional and experimental approaches to the sonnet form, each poem ultimately enacts an attempt to struggle through the anxieties of home in the hope of finding a place to love and belong.

BELLE POINT PRESS

Fort Smith, Arkansas